ALL PATHS LEAD HOME

SKY ROSHAY

ALL PATHS LEAD HOME

Poems Written by Sky Roshay
www.skyness.net

Edited by Sarahndipity Johnsen
Published by Serendipitous Entertainment
www.serendipitousentertainment.com

DEDICATION

To everyone who has ever loved me, hated me, broken my heart; stood in my way, stood up to me, stood up for me, stood up with me; danced with me, mourned with me, laughed with me, and let me do the same with them - in short, to everyone who has ever engaged with me in the richness of life.

Especially I want to thank the beings who gather in dance circles around the world for the Dances of Universal Peace, especially those who come to our retreats. May our continued communion "raise us above the distinctions and differences which divide" and may our hearts beat together as one.

Abiria
Sydrus
Barbari
Epitausa
Ausinda
Orbada
Theophila
Astacapra
Sazantium
Bardaxema
Sirastra

PART I:

THE JOURNEY BEYOND

“And David Danced Before the Lord”

In the deepest spaces of the heart,
grief and joy are one.
Dark and throbbing
brilliant ecstasy,
a screaming hush
of joyous noise
and eternal stillness:
a glimpse of the eternal mystery
too large for tears or laughter.
But the body’s every movement
ripples through the universe,
and the dance the heart knows
reaches that space beyond,
where all is One.

(7-31-97)

Untitled

In the stillness
In this moment,
only this one breath.
Past and future
fold to embrace
eternity now.
Only this one breath
and in its space,
all that is: peace.

(January 1998/May 1999)

Dancing the Razor's Edge

Open a space within yourself
to welcome whatever comes,
expecting nothing,
expecting everything.
Dance the razor's edge in
bare feet.
Ecstasy is joy and pain
mingled together.
Eventually the heart
bursts into a blaze
brighter than a million suns.
Can you believe that?
Dance and let that
guide you home.

(3-27-98)

Dancing with the Demons

When the demons come to tea
I set out mended crockery
and put music on.
And we dance to tribal beats
shouting, crying, stomping feet
in celebration;
devouring cookies and gulping warm spiced tea,
overturning chairs and lamps in our wild ecstasy.
When they came before
they gulped, devoured and overturned
in unruly passion
as I cowered and whimpered.
Now we meet in a space out of time
and dance.

(5-6-98)

Your Perfection

When you cry
do you taste in your tears
your courage to embrace your pain?
In your anger
do you feel the fire
that connects you to the stars?
When you trip
do you feel the earth
rise to cradle you in its arms?
In your joy
does your soul sing
and vibrate every cell of your being?
Do you see
the unique facets of God
that combine in you alone?
Do you know,
o beloved one,
your preciousness that makes you sacred?

(8-16-98)

Invocation

For today,
may I dance with the Divine.
May my heart beat to the rhythm of the universe;
May my breath flow with the sweet inhale of
creation and the sure exhale of dissolution.
May I feel the dance so strongly that
every step is firmly placed;
every word is rich with truth;
every act full of grace.
And may I trust so strongly that
every self-judged inadequacy
is released to the Dance as being in perfect
step, no matter what my perception is.
May the Dancer of the Universe direct the dance
through me,
and may I dance in that flow forever.

(10-9-98)

All Paths Lead Home

There are no wrong choices.
All paths lead home.
So lay down your burden
and dance. Or not, as you choose.
Be sometimes a crystal goblet,
sometimes a clay pot,
sometimes so broken
God's wine spills straight over your hands.
Perhaps your tongue needs only to remember
how to lick your fingers clean
instead of crying over spillage.
So lay down your burden
There are no wrong choices
Because all paths lead home.

(12-2, 12-13-98)

Forgiveness 2

When the sun is dropped behind the hills
its colors leak across the sky,
staining clouds and trees and air
in fiery shades of watercolor rinses
that fade in twilight's turning.
A momentary muddiness --
then, night time's splendid starkness
where points of brilliant white highlight
smudgy charcoal shadows.
This melting, spilling, moving art
we view as perfect harmony.
Might our "mistakes," in different view,
be other holy acts of grace?

(4-24-99)

The Arrival

Who are you, and where did you come from?
You have thrown my heart's garden into wild disarray.
Yesterday the flower beds were neat and orderly,
the climbing roses sedately wound around the trellis,
and the paths were clear and open.
It was safe, my garden, in its predictable beauty.
Today I see wildness everywhere:
flowers grow laughing in the middle of the path,
dandelions threaten the orderly beds,
the roses grow in tangled joy from trellis to tree
embracing all with gentle thorns.
Who are you, and where did you come from,
you who turned my heart into chaos,
who unleashed my complacency into wild abandoned
joy?

(May 18 1999)

We are born
from pieces of stars
whose dying explosions
begin the creation
of motion,
of galaxies,
of life.
Their fragments
fly through
the night and land
behind our eyes,
igniting the spark
to remind us
of the glory that we are
and how far we are from Home.

(Nov-Dec 1999)

Doing and Being

Perhaps it works like this:

You can't find God while thrashing around
determinedly through the brush
like a lost hunter seeking water buffalo tracks.
God is not yours to capture like a trophy
to hang above the mantel -
in fact, God would look pretty silly
stuffed and mounted.
Maybe, though, if you sit quietly on the grass,
cross-legged if you can manage that,
and just breathe,
God will come - if you are in stillness enough -
like a brilliant little bird with soft feathers
and bright eyes
who lands on your hand, sings to you,
and then flies into your heart.

(7-29-01)

Evening Prayer (Sky's version)

Now I lay me down to sleep,
I pray the Lord my soul to keep.
With angels watching round my bed,
at my feet and at my head,
to keep me safe thru all the night
and wake with me at break of light.

How Truth Comes

We look for truth.
Truth comes as a camel.
We were expecting a horse,
sleek and graceful,
not nearly so .... gauche.
We wait for truth.
Truth comes as a magpie.
We were expecting a songbird,
demure and melodious.
not nearly so .... raucous.
We learn.
We nod wisely.
We know Truth now.
Truth comes as a princess.
We were expecting a hag,
not nearly so ... refined.
We surrender
and simply look,
letting Truth come however it wishes.

(7-11 2003)

The Path to Enlightenment

"Awakened" is not like "asleep",
like day is not like night.
Growing slowly,
it is difficult to tell
when outlines become distinct,
when shadows separate
from shapes,
when the path becomes clear
and pitfalls are revealed
as simply shady spots
blocking the light.
And yet it happens, and all
the definitions change.
What does love mean now,
in all this brightness?

(10-18-03)

Meditation

"Go into the stillness," they said,
and so I sit, prepared.
"Coming up next!" the TV blares from the next room.
I drag my seducible curiosity away;
"stillness," I murmur.
A shattering, a small "uh-oh" from the kitchen;
I calm my hyperventilating mind;
"stillness, stillness."
A screech of tires and laughter from the street.
I tackle my inner cop and wrench it back;
"stillness, dammit, where's the freaking stillness?"

This is not, I observe quietly, very Buddha-like behavior.

Three hundred and forty seven sits later,
the two-note repertoire of bird call just outside my window
beats a counterpoint to the kids' video game
while the neighbor's lawn mower provides the drone,
and my Big Ears suddenly hear it:
the orchestra of the world, the symphony of All,
whose crescendo is
the Stillness.

(6-7-04)

God’s Fire

The angels’ wings are not celestial goose down,
white and soft and pillowy safe.
The angels’ wings are jagged fire,
colors I have no names for,
blazing flames of unfathomable splendor,
burning, burning, brighter than a million suns.
The angels’ wings beat the universe into life,
into passion, into breath, into death,
a kaleidoscope of power I cannot escape
for, lo, the angel’s wings are mine
and my flames engulf the universe
as my heart explodes, the fuel of God.

(1-20/31-05)

Love Song

When our eyes meet,
When we touch,
we dissolve.
And none of this means what you think.
If God is Love, Lover and Beloved,
who is this "I", who is this "You",
and how can This be contained
in anything smaller than a
Yes that invites in All?
Which is, of course, no container at all.
When you grasp this - which cannot be held -
and let go of all which seems familiar,
only then will your heart understand
this as a love song.

(5-6-06)

In this moment, one
Breath, and stillness, and the
Universe unfolds.

(Haiku, 11-7-13)

Letting go into
What is. A deep breath that brings
Release: Surrender.

(Haiku, 6-16-14)

Perhaps where you need to be
Isn't where you think you ought to be.
Perhaps where you need to be
Is exactly where you are, right now.
Stop for a moment,
Listen through the years to the crying
of the small child -
The one you still carry within you -
The one who was so often told
"You're too young. When we get home. Sit still. No, not now. When you're older. Don't cry.
You have to wait."
Stop for a moment. Sit.
Pull that child to you,
And know:
You are perfect as you are,
right now. No matter what.
You always have been.

(26 Feb 2017)

It could have been a poem
gathered from words hidden in the corners
of the night washed clean by rain.
But there were too few
and so I lie here and listen to the reborn world instead.

(1-10-18)

Act 738, Scene 5439

And the scene snaps to life in front of you,
Lit by a self-powered flash.
A set of emotions so hackneyed
they might as well be paint by numbers:
  Oyster grey for the sad pale face, with
  a muddy mauve for the wringing, clutching hands,
  facing a clash of red for folded arms and
  a dab of cyan for the withdrawal.
  Pale turquoise highlights for pleading,
  yellow streaks for the backward steps, the shutting down.
  A blur of pink for one last plea and a slash of black for an
abrupt departure,
  Leaving a melting puddle of sickly green grief in its wake.
As you eye the brush strokes in recognition of
the endless scenic repetition,
your mind chants "hackneyed, hackneyed"
and giggles irreverently at the word –
Hackneyed: hack kneed, hack the scene at its knees.
So it drops like a thud to the floor of your mind
and rolls over to play dead, a true comedian.
But suddenly, light – real light, not some artificially induced flash –
illuminates the scene and shifts the color scale
to broader brushstrokes.
And you see the true nature of the scene.
Magnificent tragedy twisted by rich satire; glowing
ribbons of DNA acting out millennia of human interactions,
a tapestry so rich the colors vibrate
off the palette and into your heart.
Act 1, Scene 1, an endless loop.

(3-27-18)

I can no more write a poem
than I can fly to the moon,
as if the moon and I were separate
things with space between us
rather than an infinite whole
whose wholeness is All.

(10-18-22)

PART II:

FRIENDS AND FAMILY, BITTERSWEET THROUGH THE YEARS

In the work shed's metal gloom --
eight by eight, no more --
I find my father's signature.

No sound disturbs the silence,
no breath stirs the dust.
All have long since drifted away.

Quietly I hold his tools,
wooden-handled rust.
They fit serenely in my hand.

Neat rows of cans and boxes
Unrecognized parts --
"You never know what you might need."

An empty can on the shelf,
the dry dead body
of a lizard trapped by mistake.

A victim like my father
of walls too high to scale,
in which he sought to build a life.

(April 97)

I cannot weep for all that is revealed
by what she stored away -
the pattern books proclaiming elegant clothes that could be
made for pennies when
she could barely sew;
the torn off covers of greeting cards addressed to her, meant
to someday adorn
her own simple handmade cards,
the inside messages discarded;
the lipstick containers with the bright sticks worn
down to nubs, unusable but not to be parted with;
the empty jars stored in hopes of someday filling
them with jams or savories or perhaps simply leftovers
unscorned;
the presents lovingly offered but so ill suited that she stored
them away in cupboards
too high for easy access;
the collections of screws and tapes and nails and strings
carefully sorted
out of proportion to their usefulness;
the beautiful things she wrapped up and hid away and feared
to show in daily life lest they break and cease to be beautiful.

I cannot weep for all I see here,
so little joy, so much fear and sadness,
so many longing dreams and buried hopes,
so much of life wasted within such walls.

I cannot weep, for if I started
I might never stop,
and all her pain might inhabit me forever.

(11-7-09)

My Merlyn, 1: Parting

In this peace my soul is full.
I hear its song, singing with yours.
In this space my grief meets joy
as time wraps on itself and becomes
eternity in this still moment.

Do you dream as you prepare to slip away?
Maybe as you gently breathe
(inhabiting so little physicality now)
you feel the twining of our hearts.

And when you go, will you take with you
a bit of me to cherish?
And will you leave a bit of you,
joy and laughter and love
to guide my way home?

(2-16-98)

My Merlyn, 2: Love

The third daffodil came up today -
From my window I watch them
swaying and bobbing together
in a syncopated dance,
sunlight in motion, joy in being.

The springlit sun came out today -
From the wooded path I watch it
sparkling and blinking between
the tree branches,
sunlight in motion, joy in being.

I visited your grave today
in accidental wanderings
between the sunlit trees,
musing on yellow daffodils,
and there it was:
a silent mound beneath pine boughs,
and I remembered your syncopated dance,
sunlight in motion, joy in being.
And I remembered my laughing heart,
sunlight in motion, joy in being,
stilled by a shadowed grave.

A sudden rush of emptiness,
an eternity between heartbeats.
Standing in the fullness, I see that
the daffodils dance for you,
the sunlight dances for you
and nothing loved is ever lost.
Sunlight in motion.
Joy in being.

(April 21, 1999. For Merlyn)

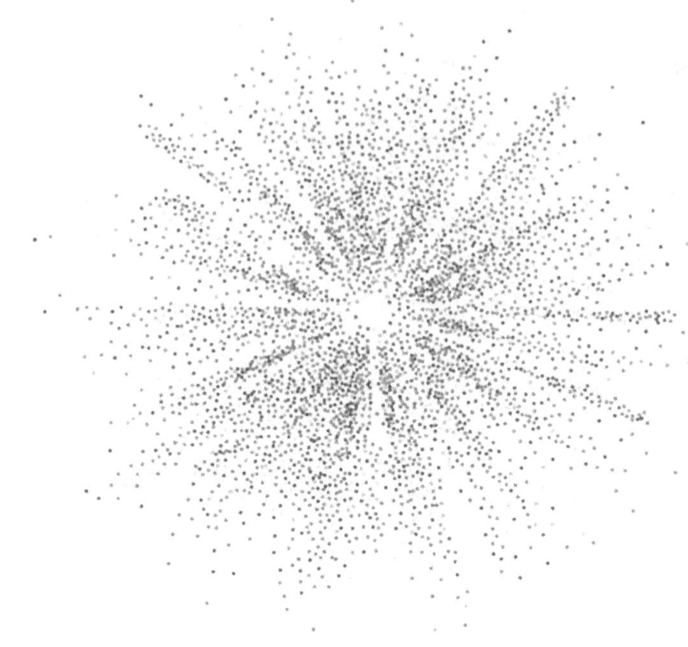

Riches

Golden nuggets spill from our tongues
and rainbows dance between our faces.
Our hugs are silken symphonies of touch
and our laughter and our tears birth
cherubs of truth
that fly away on wings of light.
Our meetings are heralded with fireworks,
and our partings leave me
wrapped in whipped cream
and floating on champagne.
Such friends I have, such friends.

(8-21-98)

To JB

The sky is brilliant with stars,
but you saw mostly darkness.
Reaching for light thru others' eyes,
you tried to believe,
but constant falls from grace eroded
faith in that elusive brightness.
Your pain flayed many
in its power and its turbulence,
and still the darkness pulled you in.
But the light has never wavered -
and that knowledge,
hidden in some deep layer of your being,
created that great struggle
instead of meek surrender.

(6-6-01)

How a Saint is Made

She was sunshine as a child,
innocent and trusting.
I hold a snapshot of her in my mind,
glowing blonde head and tiny white teeth
in a never-ending smile,
shining love like the sun.

Perhaps our mother was like that too
when she was small,
before a stern father, a young-dying mother
and the Depression
hardened her into a twisted iron bar
of disapproval and disappointment.

Mother tried to pound her shadow
into us, not knowing of course
what she was doing, hiding from it under
Christian doctrine and a sincere desire to
do right.

We suffered through it. I escaped.

My sister stayed, the sunshine fading from her
through the years of weathering
blame and rage.

Now mother is old, the light fading
from her eyes and mind,
the veneer of goodness wearing through
and the disapproval and disappointment
leaking out onto those who come around her,
mostly on my sister, who daily cares for her
and does not run away or let mother see
her tears, her anguish, the pain of the little girl
who was never good enough,
never bright enough,
who never succeeded enough to wipe away her
mother's disillusionment with the world.

And still she stays, my sister,
and aids our mother gently,
and does what she can the best she can,
though it is never good enough.

This is how a saint is made.

(12-21-07)

The Children

At a family camp last week
these two were different as sea and stone
save for gender and light brown hair.
One, an awkwardness of jutting angles,
quietly gleeful smile,
dancing carefully barefoot between the pebbles;
the other rounder and more stiffly apart,
downturned mouth and face,
scuffing noisily in flapping flops.
The eavesdropping camera, however,
captured this:
two children, one slightly taller,
standing facing each other,
one's face upturned in beatific light,
eyes closed in trust,
the other's hands,
unfolded like an opening prayer
or a budding flower to frame that face,
touching chin and cheeks like the kiss of an
angel's downy wings.
Ten years from now when they are changed
beyond recognition which will hold more truth,
moving sea and stone
or this still grace?

(8-31-05/02-09-06)

It is late in the evening
in a house where I used to live,
but fit no longer as if I have changed shape,
which perhaps I have.
The house echoes with long departed voices
mingled with childhood all
grown up and distorted.

In the morning I depart,
steering a guzzling truck west
away from the sunrise
toward the desert,
hauling my inheritance so carefully
packed and loaded.

This feels discordant,
like yanking a tree up out of the ground,
like playing at being a trucker,
like being torn between two worlds
and the past and the future.
It worries at me until I realize
my life has ever been thus,
and I relax into the paradox
and let it be what it will be,
swirling around me like smoke
and disappearing.

(11-7-09)

Heartless

Before the days of "big hair", her unruly waves framed
her head like a dark halo,
while her singular olive skin tanned and tanned,
earning her the slur "pickaninny" beside her more sedate
Southern-raised siblings and cousins.

Before the days of orthondontia,
her buck teeth stuck out;
cruel playmates taught her not to smile
or even speak.

Before the days of hospice and assisted living,
her mother died slowly;
she was the one chosen to stay home
and nurse her,
giving up an apprenticeship to a photographer and her
dreams.

She escaped to a wartime nurses' training
and career,
but panicked at the sight of blood,
making every day a torture.

She married a soldier,
best friend of her cousin's husband;
he took her half way around the world where no one
spoke her language.

She bore and raised two daughters,
and though in her family it was never spoken off,
medical records hint
at two possible miscarriages as well.

Sensitive from birth, and born before the days of
inclusivity and recognition of differences,
she was admonished to pull herself up by her non-
existent bootstraps;
little by little she withdrew into herself,
until, except on the surface,
she had nothing left to give or show or share.

She dies slowly, her mind in one piece,
her body holding up,
but her heart giving out bit by bit:
23% capacity at last measuring.

A sunset shared once, she watched the deep grey and
scarlet and said softly,
"I always wanted an evening gown in those colors."
A photo from high school, colorized, shows her slim and
tall in a gown of green.

Her heart is giving out; I only marvel it has taken so
long.

(4-25-08)

Where are the Grown Ups?

My hair is turning grey and my mother just died,
but I am not old enough to be in charge
of her funeral.
Always before, when someone died
there were adults
to follow to the church, all dressed in black,
with their hymnals and their hankies
and they knew what to say
and how to be gracious
in spite of their grief.
And we followed along
like ducklings in their wake and smiled
or lowered our eyes
and said only, “Yes, ma’am”, “thank you” and
“I love you too”
and chafed in our Sunday clothes,
dark and stiff and solemn.
Now there is no one to hide behind,
no one to rely on
to know the right words or pick the right hymns
or pay the minister and the church.
It’s only us and we aren’t old enough for this, truly.

(8 March 2009)

Warriors of the Heart

O still child,
you wandered here from some
unfathomable place
I cannot reach by Earthly means,
surrendering ageless wisdom and compassion
to inhabit a small form
beset by human frailties.
Behind the fear in your eyes,
I see the wordless courage
that fueled your choice;
the mirror of that deep knowing
reflects to me the memory
of my own choice
made so long ago.

(6-24-98)

The Spyglass

I see the children
through the wrong end of the glass,
dancing,
dancing on the sands,
shifting with the tide,
reaching to the moon for balance.
I see the children
tiny shapes,
the stars' reflection
of their own grand pattern,
watching their footprints
as they run
claiming grandeur
from the changes they force
on the sands,
shifting with the tide,
reaching to the moon for balance,
then swept away into the sea's deep mind.
I see the children
and through the wrong end of the glass
I wonder:
will we have grown in our game
at all if I move it from my eye?

(12-28-99)

New Song Melody

If I ever thought
our connection could be lost,
you just returned it to me
through the music that pours
through your heart and hands
and there are no more words
just the tears on my face
and the soaring ecstasy in my heart.

(10-14-19)

Rhythmic moving feet,
an ocean of hearts singing -
My tribe is dancing.

(Haiku, March 2013)

PART III:

OBSERVATIONS

Throw-Away Love

What a pity hearts can't be mended like clothes:
A turned collar, a darned sock;
calico patches and a border of lace.
Bright embroidery on old blue jeans.
Serene afternoons of loving care.
But alas, we have forgotten how to sew.

(6 May 97)

The silence between the notes shapes the music,
the pause between waves is the ocean's roar,
the stillness between thoughts forms the soul.

(Feb or March, 1998)

Celtic music knows
    the first ecstatic embrace of lovers,
    the heartbreak of their final parting
    and God beneath it all.

(3-17-98)

Ode to Murder Mysteries Over Real Life

Motives are layered
like onions
the centers of which
dissolve into a black hole
of incomprehension.

I have been one
blind to my own motives
as well as others'
crying onion tears
of longing to comprehend.

The world does not make sense.
Motives are not clear.
Groundlessness trips us.

This is why murder mysteries are so satisfying.

(1-3-23)

She donned her glasses
and fell asleep
and did not wake
so when they found her
she seemed studious
rather than dead, an
enviable end.

(1-16-19)

God does nothing.
God is everything.

(10-18-03)

This being human is such a playground
where all our joys and sorrows
parade past in gaudy velvet and glass beads,
noisy on the melodramatic stage of illusion,
capturing our attention like wide-eyed children,
while all that is important
drifts by
on the gentle breeze
and in the soft shadows of sunlight.

(June 15ish 2000)

We are born into this world,
each of us delivered clean and new
as a love note from the Divine,
messages of compassion and peace
written clearly on our hearts.

Then life happens.
Shredded and battered
our hearts still hold,
flapping bravely in the wind
like tattered prayer flags.

(5-30-06)

Perhaps it is the role of poets
to hold the grief of the world,
plunging its depths,
examining its pores,
lifting it to the light of day
instead of letting it sit,
inert,
hidden from the world
that is fearful of its beauty.

(6-22-06)

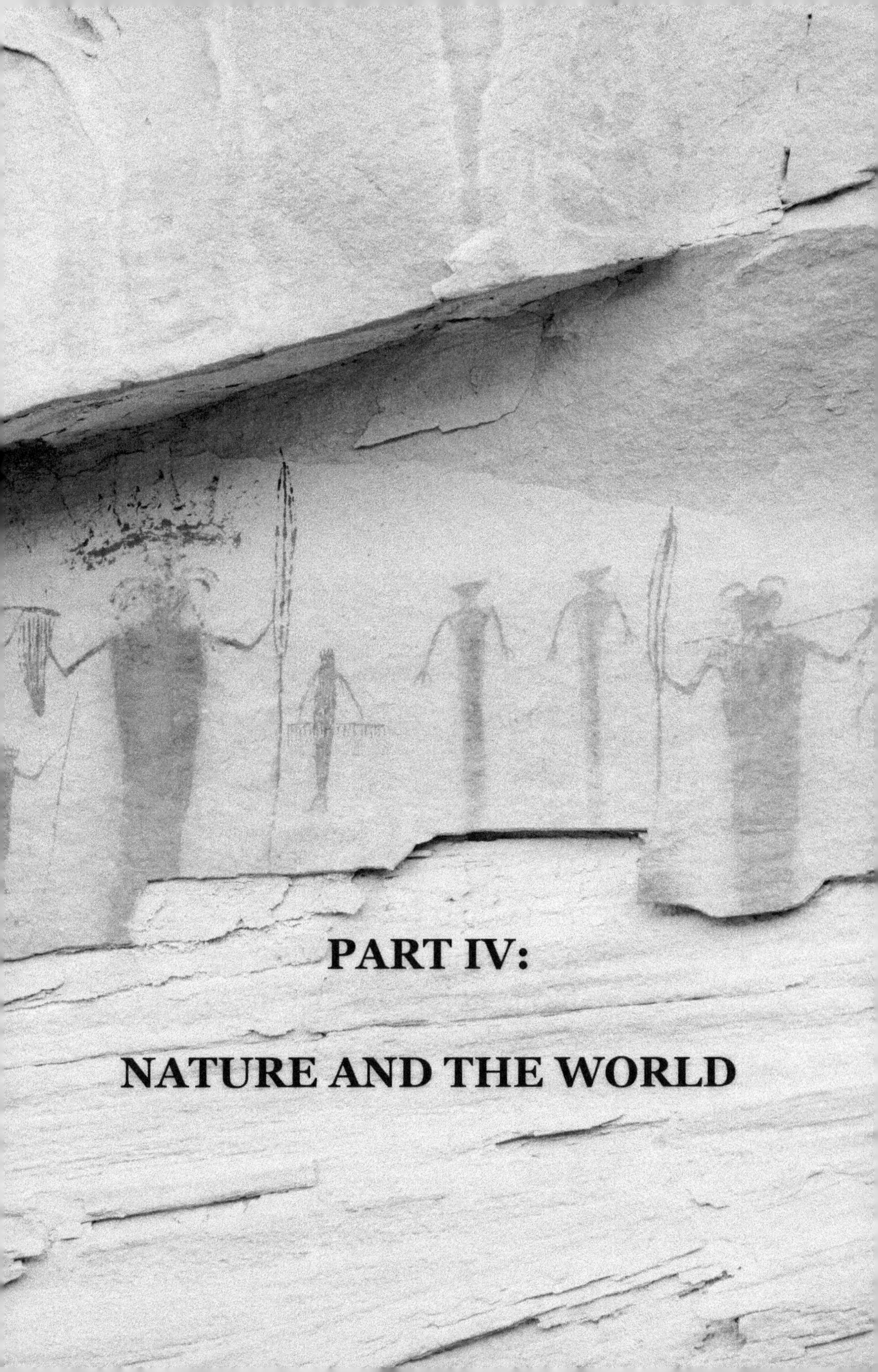

PART IV:

NATURE AND THE WORLD

When I Dance

When I dance
with the stars in my arms,
I breathe in
ecstasy.

When I lie
in the hollow of a hill,
I dream
protected.

When I sing
with the chorus of the wolves,
I thrill in
harmony.

When I listen
with a hush in my heart
to the breathing of the earth,
then I know
I'm home.

(3-31-97)

The Dance

When flickers of sunlight
dance between aspen leaves
to land on my face,
my heart explodes
like a dandelion puff,
scattering love and joy
to sail to a million distant places,
and return to me
in flickers of sunlight
that dance between
the aspen leaves.

(6-24-98)

The snowflakes dance a graceful glide,
giggling their way to the ground.
They care not for schedules or snow tires,
only the gleeful joy of their spiral dance
onward toward the One,
the great snowbank of Life
that gently melds individuals into the whole.

Do you seek a parallel?
Ponder not, lest thinking melt your brain.

Simply dance
Grieving not over schedules or snow tires.
Simply dance, and all will unfold in grace.

(5-1-99)

Canyonlands

Let the light cleanse me,
let the breeze feed me;
let the stars tickle the colors of my soul.

Let feet caress the Mother,
let eyes caress each other;
let hearts join as One in this Circle of the Whole.

(1-30-02)

The coyote chorus crackles,
breaking its notes into bite sized pieces -
scorning the traditional form,
the expected display -
and chuckles wildly
at the world's inability
to understand its music,
while the stars whirl
in a dizzy dance,
at one with the troubadours
of the cosmos.

(Sept 2005)

I woke early in my tent
securely held by the earth
and alive to the tips of my toes.
I walk silently on sand slipping
between sage bushes and onto
slick rock sandstone.
The land breathes with me,
the birds speak of me,
the breeze touches me with curiosity.
A highway marks one corner of my paradise;
every so often the sound of a car drifts
toward me like an echo from a
parallel universe: it has nothing to do with me.
And even were a sharp eyed alien to spot me
(though I dress in desert sand and faded green)
and their consciousness extend toward me,
like tentacles to trap me in that other world,
I would be unaffected,
rooted as I am,
protected as I am,
in birdsong and sagebrush
and sculpted rock and sand,
The silence born of presence.

(9-26-10)

Call to Prayer

I am neighbors to the geese,
I in my house, they on their sandbar in the river.
I have watched them through
the spring and summer
hatching eggs and raising fluff balls.
They have, perhaps, watched me
come and go on foot and in my car,
while not preoccupied with goosely lore:
    how to swim in a regally straight single file,
    to dunk and bathe without filling one's nostrils
    with water,
    to amphibiously lift off and land with a
    semblance of grace and no midair stalls,
    to raise one's voice in full measure
    amidst the whole.

Now, in the autumn light they rest, motionless on
their sandbar,
content with their labors and the success thereof.

In between my own labors, I watch them
 soaking up the sun, bathing in the air,
 living in the elusive shimmer of this moment's
 perfection.

Five times a day, perhaps, or more,
in a wave of fullness,
they rise,
an unmelodious multiphonic hallelujah chorus.
Beating their wings against the air,
they rise in a graceful spiral that circles
over my house, over the trees
and the cows and the bumpy country road
and the cyclists intent
on the ground beneath their wheels,
drawing us all in close.

Five times a day they rise,
a reminder, a call to prayer,
and I stop my labors
and my soul replies,
"Amen".

(10-7-05)

The snow falls silent
The world drifts away in white
And so do the words.

(Haiku, 2-5-21)

Owls glide on silent
Feathers, slicing through the night –
Ghostly claws of change.

(Haiku, 9-27-14)

Hummingbird outside the window.
Morning stillness and warmth.
The world breathes softly,
waiting for potential to unfold...

(8-9-09)

We sit on our evening patio
carved from the hillside
watching the night arrive.
One twinkling light far across the valley,
the neighbor's seven cows,
dark floating blobs in the field below.
We slap at mosquitoes until the bat comes,
swooping rapidly by our heads in a delicate
mosquito eating dance.
The stars shyly appear,
in ones and twos and more.
The moon is late.
The crickets drone over the silence
and the music of the spheres.
We sit in wonder,
grateful for it all.
Especially the bat.

(20-21 Aug 09)

Early morning light
the color of stillness with
overtones of gold.

(Haiku, 9-9-09)

It seems impossible at night that this dirt track
could take us home,
embedded as it is in the land of shadows
that stretches to infinity,
hiding magic shapes and lands –
Elephants, Arabia, UPS trucks, Middle Earth.
But at twilight the shapes are real,
grounded in this earth,
and so this lone cow faces me beside the track,
its back to the icy wind.
The rancher has not run cows here for weeks;
is this a solitary bovine, left and forgotten?
Or, in the gathering gloom, is this shape
a projection from those other realms,
a placid black rhinoceros with blobby white spots?

(1-18-10)

Utah's Canyon Country

This breeze has not blown through a city;
it does not carry the smell of exhaust
or the sound of traffic,
it has not bounced off of steel or concrete
or been funneled down unnatural chasms.

This breeze rustles the cottonwood leaves
and caresses the red rocks as it flows over them;
it ripples the surface of desert streams
and carries the bird calls across the valleys.

Here in its home the breeze is content,
and so am I.
It knows its place in this vastness
and if I follow the breeze, so do I.

(5-19-08)

Leaving Baja

The early morning breeze is brisk with winter.
The pale sunlight offers warmth
conjured mostly from the memory
of other sunrises more obliging.
Unpacked, repacking, moving onward again,
the rhythm of this day no different from
the ones that came before,
except for the final destination so far
from this land that holds its heart in its smile.
The magic holds though,
as it has held through each counted day of
this caravan journey,
and so I carry that with me
and that will sustain me
until I can return again.

(16 Feb/16 Aug 09)

Ode to Food, with Apologies to Rumi

This one eats only fruit
and looks very healthy.
This one revels in chocolate
and laughs a lot.
This one inhales meat and carbs
and runs marathons.

They say to drink a lot of water
(they also say it can be overdone).
They say do not, do not eat fats
(except for these special healthy ones).
They say to avoid all kinds of things:
    dairy, wheat, sugar, meat;
    grains, tomatoes, fried potatoes;
    soft drinks, chips, beer and dips;
    these too cooked, those too raw;
    pickles, tofu and cole slaw;
    caffeine, peanuts, mushrooms, wine
    and brussel sprouts.

Whatever can one do?
Perhaps the only way through
is to die.

(8-12-05)

Night Truth

Darkness palpable
conceals a doorway;
coyotes howl
my blood pulses in counterpoint.
Ancestors' drums echo.
We spark a light
the door opens –
a thousand bright miracles.

Only fear sustains the dark.

(10-29-13)

Gardening is a Lot Like Life

Something has eaten all the lettuce.
Something else has chopped down
the tomato plants and carried them off -
it can't be the same "something"
or with all this sustenance it would
be as big as an elephant,
and surely we would have noticed that.

The gourd plant has sprouted a tentacle
that has grown through the fence
and seems to be headed for town,
ten miles away.

The carrots, after a slow start, are sprouting,
not just in their beds, but also in the pathway,
making it difficult to approach them.

The grape vine is putting all its energy into "vine"
rather than "grape".

A squash plant is growing exuberantly
from within the confines of a cinder block,
which now cannot be seen beneath the greenery.

The radishes are growing like weeds,
leaving us to wonder
just exactly what does one do with 25 pounds of radishes?

Has anyone seen the onions?
We did plant them, didn't we?

The flowers raise their faces to the sun,
and we all rejoice,
even the feisty hummingbirds.

The pepper plants are in their glory,
mourning the absence of their salsa partners.

So much movement,
so much life,
so many unexpected blessings
and dashed hopes,
such a green reflection of life.

(7-26-07)

Offering: God's Video Camera

Around the mesa and down the deserted road,
I took a walk.
It was happy to be taken, as was the dog, whose
accompaniment was never doubted
by any of us.

My eyes drank in all the shades of spring green,
garnished with flowers wild in every hue,
as good for me as any spinach
or other leafy greens.

My skin soaked in the sunlight, vitamin D and
something more –
the warmth of a lover's gaze, perhaps.

Deer had ambled by in the night,
leaving only split hoofed tracks.

A lizard scampered through the dust,
leaving an ecstatic score of tracks
like music I can't yet read.
And clearly, clearly, in the stillness
I hear my footsteps crunch
on the packed sandy track,
and the birds, at least a dozen tribes,
calling serenely, each in its own way,
"All is well."

In a jolt, I understood:
I am God's video camera.

God and the angels gather on the other side
to incorporeally experience the corporeal world,
through me.

What do I wish to offer them
(who are really One, the All-That-Is, everywhere)?

Shall I offer drunken laughter,
angry shouting and Unkind actions,
self-pitying wallows?

Or shall I offer love,
like solitary walks on serene mornings,
full of the awareness of majesty?

(5-31-12)

Watching the sun come up
the sky glides from pale absence of color
to pastel blue with mango flavored edges -
A daily miracle that happens quietly,
with no fanfare,
just the repeated solitary offering of beauty,
whether anyone sees it or not.

Maybe that is what we need to offer to the world:
Our own sunrise,
no matter what the world offers back – or doesn't.

(April 2020)

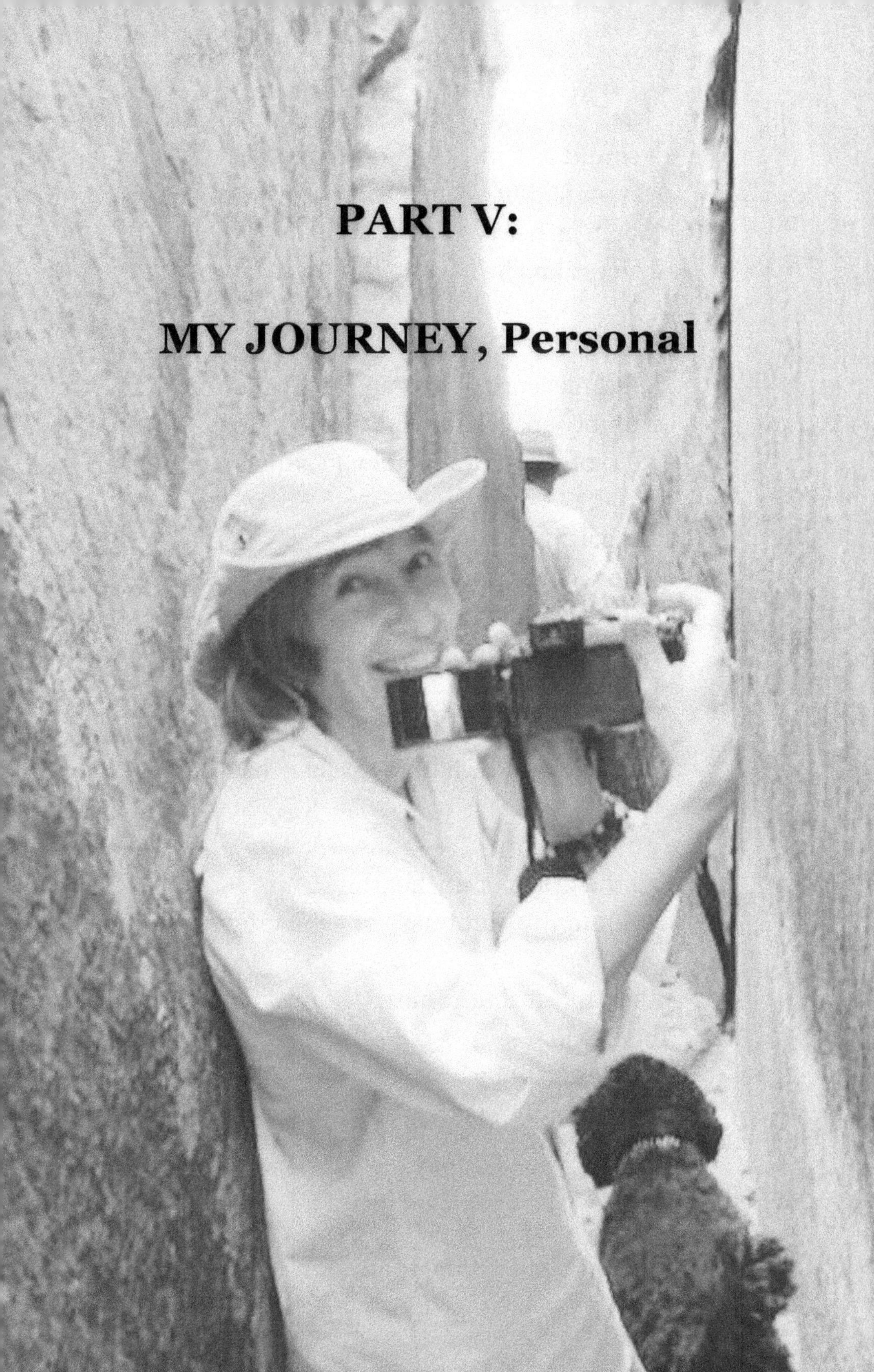

PART V:

MY JOURNEY, Personal

“Grief”
: a sound as soft
as snow sliding from a roof;
: a pain as heavy
as an avalanche’s white thunder.

Grief
: a full measure of loss and regret --
an empty space in the pattern of life,
a void of now un-ask-able questions.

This grief
gathers other griefs,
as geese gather
to honk and splash and disturb the calm.
My tears,
droplets shaken free of their pond,
fall for you and what might have been.

You
: all the griefs of my heart
frozen in the numbness of my winter.

When the spring comes,
in its time,
the geese will fly,
trailing feathers.
I will gather them,
a soft nest
for my heart
in the warmth of the thaw.

Before a Phoenix

I sit alone in the deepening dark,
a pile of bones bewildered by the change.
In hatred's fire, I was the fuel
burned for touching the sun
which set on the charred remains.

Sifting through the ashes, I find bones
which ache at the wind's touch.
I have no softness to protect me,
no sustenance to offer those who come near,
only bones that rattle of death and dryness.

(12 April 97)

Our eyes ignited candles, lighting up my heart,
reaching out to touch the stars with trembling awe.
Full of grace and light, a promise for eternity:
my beloved in the universe's stars,
the universe in my beloved's eyes.

What makes the stars go out?
What turns the light to dark?
What demons in my soul awoke to feed the fire of fear
and tumble me from ecstatic heights?

A crazy spiraled fall,
rage, grief and fear spat into your face like some
unholy ballast
that did not save me in the end.
I fired the rage at you
(not completely blameless though you are)
in futile desperation to jettison my pain.
Maddening grief beat the bars of my sanity,
and my faith in the stars stretched taut --
but did not break...

Grief still drips in my heart, but the flood has passed.
My hands fumble and tremble
searching for the candle that must be there,
to light myself this time
and reach the stars reflected in my eyes:
Beloved.

(8-3-97)

Meet Me There

Sometimes fear outsings my soul:
Listen past it. Meet me there
where the glowing spark becomes the whole.
Listen gently. Meet me there.

My soul's love song fuels that spark:
Hear it singing? Meet me there
where love expands and lights the dark,
ever singing. Meet me there.

Yes, we stumble, sometimes stunned,
spinning wildly into fear.
I can stand there and not run,
if you can. Can you meet me there?

Each soul does its own song sing:
Seeking harmony.
Meet me there in that space
where we can sing together. Meet me there.

And I promise if you stand
true and open come what may,
I will true and open stand
to meet you and not back away.
Meet me there.

(19-20 Feb 98)

Prayer of Gratitude

Thank you God for all I have
and all the blessings yet to come today.
And thanks a lot for the things I don't have
that I never wanted anyway.

(6-10-98)

Flailing, I let go
when the center did not hold.
Now, all form is gone.

(Haiku, Dec 98)

Stumbling through the dark,
shadowboxing with the night --
-- will this path lead home?

(Haiku, Dec 98)

That One Question

This morning when I awoke
I don't know if I knew who I was or not.
(I didn't ask that question of myself, you see)
Instead I lay, wrapped in silk and flannel,
a cozy cocoon coming to new life,
and wondered,
"What day is it? What am I supposed to do today?"
A million universes of opportunity lost,
in that one question!
But wait, all is not lost
for now I sit here writing and humming to myself,
content and glowing
and this is not part of the answer I contrived to that one question!

Tomorrow when I awaken,
wrapped in silk and flannel,
another cozy cocoon coming to new life,
perhaps I'll ask,
"Who am I, really?"
or
"How am I to be in God, today?"
And perhaps a million universes
will blaze into existence.
Or perhaps, I'll write another poem.
Or perhaps not.
It matters not: it's all God no matter how we ask it.

(3-29-99)

Heavenly light
wrap me in bliss,
yet stay my hand
to say but this
and no more:

I would not make
another choice
in spite of pain
so long in voice
from before;
for all those trials
have served me well
and brought me here
in Light to dwell --
Beloved.

(5-25-99)

Grace Notes

In these blessed moments
my heart stills
like a mountain wildflower lifting its light to the sky,
singing its song with all its grace.
In these moments
the discords die,
leaving the purity of my heart song.
And as I listen,
grace notes gather
to ripple out and bless all
that have made my heart song that which it is
in these blessed moments.

(8-26-99)

Hu I AM

I am the Sky
bridge between
heaven and earth
ever-changing seeming,
serenely constant being,
keeper of the space
for dreams and flight.

I am the Mystic
born of the depths,
moonlight and shadow
dancing on the earth.
Sophia's wisdom
sun blind
in pragmatic day.

I am the Weaver
twining the words
of souls and hearts
into a tapestry
deeper than death
woven of God strands
delighting in the pattern.

Hu amongst hu
I AM.

(Sept 21-22 1999)

The skies fall on me
breaking me open.
All of me has spilled out,
and now I wait for the heavens to pour in.

(Nov? 1999)

Inebriated,
cacophonated -
the Teacher said,
"Learn to be a rishi in the city,"
but which God would I hear
singing there?

(2002?)

Peace and Prayer and Pain

A day of crystal,
so sharp it cuts,
a silence so vast
it is the space
between God's heartbeats.

A meadow,
surrounded by white powder slopes,
bright with snow and sun and stillness.
I am rolling down the hill
naked.

(10-26-04)

Presence

I can remember so little of the world's turnings -
what makes a car go,
how the numbers add up,
why politeness matters,
who was in love with whom -
now I remember only
the golden light of a fall evening,
the caress of a friend,
the smell of lavender, and chocolate,
the presence of God.

(10-29, 30-04)

Brilliance

I have abandoned the words,
shaken them from me
like brittle twigs and limp leaves
gathered as I've walked through the underbrush.
Now in the expanse of light
I breathe, wordless,
and let it all come.
There is no more to say.

(7-26-07)

I will arise now and go,
and if I were to look back
I would see all my burdens and worries
puddled in a heap where I sat
for so long.

Ahead of me is light
and music and
a breeze fragrant with birdsong and jasmine.
So, I will not look back.
I will arise now and go.

(7-14-09)

The circle comes together
like laundry comes to the washer –
stained and tired, dusty and worn.
God's grace pours down like water,
the chanting soap, the blissful bleach.
We turn and spin, we chant God's name.
Rinsed in joy, cleansed in light,
We emerge like new
Wearing our selves like clean laundry.

(7-16-11)

On Turning Fifty Eight

Turning thirty, the great milestone, the end of an era:
It is too late now to become the youngest author of the Great American Novel,
The youngest billionaire
owner of a successful dot com,
An Olympic medal winner of almost anything.
Goodbye to childhood, studenthood, commitmentlessness:
The only prizes now are of the more adult kind,
as yet mostly unknown and probably really boring.
I myself had no trouble turning thirty;
having looked ahead, I panicked at twenty-nine,
So much so that I faced thirty with an exhausted ease.
Now I face twice that many years,
and I have still not written the Great American Novel
or become a billionaire (the Olympics were never in the running).
That is probably good for my ego,
which has to content itself with other,
less tangible prizes:
I am often kind to my husband,
I care about my friends,
I live with a small carbon footprint,
and I have learned to be aware of Love.
Perhaps these are prizes not so small,
nor attainable half a lifetime ago.

(3-10-12)

A Poor Attempt at What Lies Beyond Words

Powerful gold-white connection
at the level of absolute source
so strong, so profound it cannot be broken.
We came here to help each other
remember we are safe
we are loved.
So even though our ego selves
have gotten in the way,
the love and the connection
cannot be broken.
You are safe, you are loved.
As am I.
So even in the grief
all is well.

(11-17-22)

Beach Poem: Don't Give Up, Kid

Twelve years old, long hair tangled in her face,
skinny, awkward in her bones, she
slips silently out the door
in the early morning light,
A boundless soul trapped in a small body,
small house, small life,
desperate to escape,
hoping to see a sunrise, a squirrel,
a different world.
Circumscribing the small yard
of the small house
in an endless suburb,
sunrise is hidden by the houses, the trees,
the closed-in life.
So she imagines a glory seen only in photographs,
imagines walking woodland paths
and rocky heights,
fording wide streams and dancing in the surf,
none of which exist within many miles of her suburban
prison.
Even the nearest park is several miles away but
she doesn't wander far,
fearing her mother's wrath,
which can strain the whole household,
and this small self cannot carry the burden of so much
guilt.

So now, some fifty years later,
in a thicker body, shorter tangled hair,
still awkward in these bones,
I step silently out a door
to face the boundless glory of sunrise.
Mountains, desert, ocean beach –
no matter where I stand
I send a prayer to her
and hope that my standing here
is proof that she has heard.
(2-14-2015)

This Evening's Rumination, Just Because

Sometimes, in the summer evenings,
I sit on the brick patio in front of the hillside house,
and I watch the dog splashing in his wading pool
and the cat lying on a propped up board as if on a point
overlooking a cliff,
and I watch the light change
on the hill across the valley,
and I feel the magnificence of the earth's rotating as it
hurls through space,
and I also feel the deep center of stillness that lies
beneath all this motion;
and in those moments
I have no need of practices,
which seem to, with words, artificially create the sense of
infinite eternity that I am within:
I am content with the actuality and all is well.

(6/23/16)

The Ineffable

"I" am fighting for "my" life,
hoping to lose.
I-me-my-mine – heavy weights
that drag "me" down
drowning.

Letting go, buoyant consciousness arises,
a still, strong center.
Centered everywhere = nowhere = all the same.

Fear, the last clutching,
vigilant, determinedly
babbling stories to
keep "me" safe.
Still the buoyant consciousness arises.
Eventually it will envelop even that.

(12-23-22)

Requiem: Santa Fe Vision, with Postlude

Santa Fe night scene, 1994:
A successful folk singer, long admired,
striding down the street with her companion
in and out of shadows.
She blonde, he dark, but otherwise matched –
long black wool coats, tight black pants,
black boots and instrument cases,
so cool, confident, comfortable with each other,
glamorous and magical.

"I want that!" I cried, with more longing
than I knew I possessed.
It burst my soul, searing it,
a snapshot of the impossible:
pristine, revered, treasured.
Twenty five years later
the impossible became real,
manifest (except for all that black),
glorious and magical.

I wanted it to be larger than it already was.
I reached too far.
Unbalanced, I fell.

The vision shattered, sharp shards
mingling with the tattered shreds of my heart.
The real, now sinking back into
unreachable impossibility,
as in vain I try to piece it back together.

It's time to sweep it all up,
dust pan to dust bin.

Let it go.

Brittle maya shattering my perceptions:
a story, a dream, an illusion.
(1-14-24)

Postlude (9-28-24):
Yes, Icarus dreamed.
And fell. And died.
But oh, the glory and magic
of that short flight.
I dreamed, I flew, I fell –
but I did not die.
Is it better/worse to nurse a shattered heart
or die in the fullness
of fulfillment?

I have no answers yet.

SKY ROSHAY

Hu I Am

I am the Sky
bridge between
heaven and earth
ever-changing seeming,
serenely constant being,
keeper of the space
for dreams and flight.

I am the Mystic
born of the depths,
moonlight and shadow
dancing on the earth
Sophia's wisdom
sunblind
in pragmatic day.

Note: "Hu" is a Sufi term for the beginning and end of all sound, the equivalent of "Om". This particular aspect of it lives in a cob house at the end of a dirt road outside Snowflake, AZ and travels a lot as a leader and musician for the Dances of Universal Peace.

As a leader, musician, and mentor for the Dances of Universal Peace, Sky has been organizing and staffing at Dance camps in the United States and Mexico since 1999. She also facilitates "Deeper Dance" conversations at camps, where the synergistic wisdom of participants reveals wisdom about the energy and practice of the Dances, their role in our lives, and the way they can anchor spiritual truths into our way of being in the world and transform our reality.

Sky focuses on collaborating with other Dance leaders, and leaders of other spiritual practices, to offer co-created retreats believing strongly in the power and wisdom of community. We all bring wisdom to the circle to share.

Her other interests include playing guitar, writing poetry, traveling and boon dock camping with friends, and hiking to rock art and ancient sites in the American Southwest. With Dennis Roshay, Sky co-produces videos on rock art and ancient sites. Their home is an off-grid cob house in rural Arizona that they built. They both enjoy caring for the property (and SamDog, who shares many of the adventures), preparing for the next travel, and watching the movement of light and seasons across the landscape.

www.skyness.net

ALL PATHS LEAD HOME

www.ingramcontent.com/pod-product-compliance
Lightning Source LLC
LaVergne TN
LVHW010936110826
845149LV00013B/2624

* 9 7 9 8 9 9 3 3 9 8 5 3 2 *